PLAY IT IN SPANISH

In this compilation are presented selections from some of the finest games and songs of assembled folklore in the Spanish language. It is hoped that they will be received with special pleasure not only by the reader who collects games and songs for children, but more especially by the children themselves.

Learning a language can be fun and interesting, more so if it is an exchange among children of some of the things they love to do the most: play games!

These songs and games for the elementary school child are intended to give the English-speaking boy or girl a first understanding of another language; for the child of Spanish heritage they may serve as a reminder of a rich background and culture.

PLAY IT
in
SPANISH

*Spanish Games and Folk Songs
for Children*

Collected by Mariana Prieto

Music by Elizabeth Colwell Nielsen

Illustrated by Regina and Haig Shekerjian

The John Day Company • New York

An Intext Publisher

Library of Congress Cataloging in Publication Data

Prieto, Mariana Beeching de   comp.
    Play it in Spanish.

    SUMMARY: *Seventeen games and action songs from Latin America, Spain, and the West Indies including the music for the songs and the words in Spanish with a free English translation.*
        English and Spanish.
        1. Singing games, Spanish.   2. Singing games, Spanish American.   [1. Singing games.   2. Games.   3. Folk songs, Spanish.   4. Folk songs, Spanish American]   I. Nielsen, Elizabeth Colwell, 1900-   II. Shekerjian, Regina, illus. III. Shekerjian, Haig, illus.   IV. Title
    [GV1215.P75]   793.4   79-140474
    ISBN: 0-381-99726-X

The John Day Company, 257 Park Avenue South, New York, N.Y. 10010

Published on the same day in Canada by Longman Canada Limited.

Printed in the United States of America
Designed by The Etheredges

NOTES TO THE READER

Verses set to old tunes tell little stories and a folk song grows. No one knows the source of a true folk song. It is interpreted by the children who sing it and the games that they play as it is sung. These Spanish games have been played, and the songs sung, for more years than it is possible to remember. Some of the songs are so old that people differ on how and where they originated. These are gay, happy action songs that invite movement as they are sung. The games that go with them are described here and a free English translation of the verses is given. Usually the games are played or danced in circle formation.

It is suggested that the lyrics of the songs be read aloud slowly several times to become familiar with the Spanish words, before trying to sing them to the music.

The melody is separated from the piano music so that it is easier to read the syllables of each Spanish word with the notes they match.

Free English translations are given.

This material can be played on the bells by following the melody. It is suitable for guitar, banjo or autoharp by playing the chords written in the piano music. A rhythm band could accompany this music, bringing out the time by accenting the primary and secondary beats, according to the interpretation of the director.

CONTENTS

DUÉRMETE MI NIÑO (CANCIÓN DE CUNA)

Sleep, My Child (Cradle Song)

(Central America)

This is a lullaby that little girls sing when they rock their dolls to sleep. Mothers sing it too when they put their small babies to sleep.

It is called an *arrullo* (lullaby) or *canción de cuna* (cradle song). It has the lilting quality of a sleepy-time tune. It can be a role-playing song as children act it out.

Duérmete mi niño   Sleep, my child
Duérmete mi amor   Sleep, my love
Duérmete pedazo   Sleep, little piece of my heart.
De mi corazón.

Este niño lindo   This pretty child
Que nació de día   Who was born in daytime
Quiere que lo lleven   Wants to be taken
A la dulcería.   To the candy store.

Este niño lindo   This pretty child
Que nació de noche   Who was born at night
Quiere que lo lleven   Wants to be taken
A pasear en coche.   For a ride in a coach.

DUÉRMETE MI NIÑO (CANCIÓN DE CUNA)

Duér-me-te mi ni - ño Duér-me-te mi a-mor Duér-me-te pe-da - zo

De mi co-ra-zón. Es-te ni-ño lin-do Que na-ció de dí-a

Quie-re que lo lle-ven A la dul-cer-í-a. Es-te ni-ño lin-do

Que na-ció de no-che Quie-re que lo lle-ven A pa-sear en co-che.

Arranged by Elizabeth Colwell Nielsen

EL JUEGO DEL PAÑUELO

The Handkerchief Game

(Mexico)

A list of actions should be written on the chalkboard, or a chart hung up for all to see:

Vamos a bailar.	Let us dance.
Vamos a patinar.	Let us skate.
Vamos a brincar.	Let us jump.
Vamos a cantar.	Let us sing.
Vamos a volar.	Let us fly.

A standing line of boys forms; facing them, a standing line of girls.

The boy at the head of the line takes a large *pañuelo* (handkerchief) and makes a big knot in each corner. He then chooses which action he wishes to perform.

To start the game, the boy is blindfolded with another handkerchief.

The music is played as the boy walks down the line facing the girls and drops the knotted *pañuelo* in front of one of them. He removes the blindfold to see whom he has chosen. She becomes his partner and puts on her head the knotted *pañuelo* that the boy dropped at her feet.

The boy invites the girl to join him in the action decided on, as for example, he says:

"*Vamos a patinar.*" (Let us skate.)

The girl replies, "*Con mucho gusto.*" (With much pleasure.)

They join hands and go through the motions of skating. To the music they skate to the end of the line, back to the beginning and then down to the end again to complete their action. The next boy at the head of the line then takes the *pañuelo* and begins his turn.

The pattern is repeated until all the children have had turns.

EL JUEGO DEL PAÑUELO

Original composition by Elizabeth Colwell Nielsen   19

EL CONEJO DE ESPERANZA

The Rabbit of Hope

(Cuba)

For this game the children form a moving circle but do not hold hands. One child is the *conejo* (rabbit). The *conejo* stands inside the circle and is blindfolded. He tries to catch one of the other children and this one he is allowed to tag or kiss. The child he catches then becomes the *conejo* and the procedure is repeated. All the children sing the song as they walk in the circle.

Lindo conejo Esperanza,
Salió desde esta mañana,
Y a las doce ha de venir.
Y aquí está, el conejo aquí está
Y besarás a la que tu quieras más.

Pretty rabbit of Hope
Went out this morning,
At twelve o'clock he should come back.
And here he is! The rabbit is here.
And he will kiss the one that
He loves best!

20

EL CONEJO DE ESPERANZA

Lin - do co - ne - jo Es - pe - ran - za, Sa - lió des - de es-ta ma - ña - na,

Y a las do - ce ha de ve - nir. Y a - quí es-tá, el co -

ne - jo a - quí es-tá Y be - sa - rás a la que tu quie - ras más.

Moderato

Arranged by Elizabeth Colwell Nielsen

PEPITO

(Cuba)

This song is sung as the children form two lines. Two of them hold their hands high, joining them to form a "bridge." The others pass under the bridge, singing the song. When the bridge is lowered and one child is caught, he becomes Pepito. He then steps aside and is out of the game. This procedure and singing continue until each child has had a chance to be caught and to be Pepito. Then the game ends.

Mamá, papá,	Mamá, Papá,
Pepito se quiere casar	Peter wants to marry
Con una viudita	With a little widow
De la capital.	From the capital.
Urí, urí, urá,	Urí, Urí, Urá,
Pepito se casará.	Peter wants to marry.

22

PEPITO

Ma - má, ____ pa - pá, ____ Pe - pi - to se quie - re ca - sar. ____

Con u - na viu - di - ta ____ De la ca - pi - tal. ____

U - rí, u - rí, u - rá, ____ Pe - pi - to se ca - sa - rá. ____

Arranged by Elizabeth Colwell Nielsen

AL ÁNIMO

Cheer Up

(Central America)

This is a song that children sing when they play "Cheer Up!" They all form a circle and join hands, while one child, the *reina* (queen) or *rey* (king), remains outside. As they skip around, the *reina* or *rey* tries to get into the circle by bending down low and getting under the other children's joined hands.

Al ánimo, al ánimo,	Cheer up, cheer up,
La fuente se rompió.	The platter has broken.
Al ánimo, al ánimo,	Cheer up, cheer up,
Mandarla a componer.	Get them to fix it.
Al ánimo, al ánimo,	Cheer up, cheer up,
No tenemos dinero.	We have no money.
Al ánimo, al ánimo,	Cheer up, cheer up,
Nosotros le daremos.	We will give it to you.
Al ánimo, al ánimo,	Cheer up, cheer up,
De qué se hace el dinero?	With what do you make money?
Al ánimo, al ánimo,	Cheer up, cheer up,
De cáscara de huevo.	With the shell of an egg.
Urí, urí, urá,	Hurrah, hurrah, hurrah,
La reina va a pasar.	The queen is going to pass.
Los de adelante corren mucho,	Those in front must run a lot
Y los de atrás se quedarán.	So those behind will be left!

24

AL ÁNIMO

1. Al á - ni - mo, al á - ni - mo, La fuen-te se rom-pi - ó.
2. Al á - ni - mo, al á - ni - mo, Man-dar-la a com-pon - er.
3. Al á - ni - mo, al á - ni - mo, No te - ne-mos di - ne - ro.
4. Al á - ni - mo, al á - ni - mo, No - so-tros le dar-em - os.
5. Al á - ni - mo, al á - ni - mo, De qué'se hace' el di - ne - ro?
6. Al á - ni - mo, al á - ni - mo, De cas-ca - ra de hue - vo.

U - rí, u - rí, u - rá, La rei - na va a pa - sar. Los de

a - de - lan - te co - rren mu - cho, Y los de a - trás se que - da - rán.

PIANO
Lively

Arranged by Elizabeth Colwell Nielsen

PARA SUBIR AL CIELO

To Get to Heaven

(Cuba)

This is a song that children sing as they march.

Para subir al cielo,
Se necesita
Una escalera grande
Y otra chiquita.

To get to heaven
You need
A large ladder
And another small one.

PARA SUBIR AL CIELO

Pa - ra su - bir al cie - lo, Se ne - ce - si - ta, U -

na es - ca - le - ra gran - de Y'o - tra chi - qui - ta.

Arranged by Elizabeth Colwell Nielsen

YO TENGO UNA MUÑECA

I Have a Little Doll

(Spain)

In Spain beautiful regional costumes are worn for the folk dances. These dances and songs are taught to the children and the costumes are handed down from one generation to the next. For example, Andalusia is famous for its laces and lace stockings.

This is a song to sing about a doll. Little girls in Spanish countries have sung it for many centuries. It is so old no one can really remember who wrote it. This is a gesture song, the singers pointing to each article of clothing as they sing.

Yo tengo una muñeca,	I have a little doll
Vestida de azul	With a dress of blue
Con zapatos blancos,	And white shoes
Y camisón de tul.	And a petticoat of tulle
Las medias caladas,	With stockings of lace
De estilo andaluz,	In Andalusian style
Sombrerito blanco,	A little white hat
Y su canesú.	And an undershirt.

YO TENGO UNA MUÑECA

Yo ten-go u na mu-ñe-ca, Ves-ti-da de a-zul
Con za-pa-tos blan-cos, Y ca-mis-ón de tul. Las
me-di-as ca-la-das, De es-ti-lo'an-da-luz,
Som-brer-i-to blan-co, Y su ca-ne-sú.

PIANO
Moderato

Arranged by Elizabeth Colwell Nielsen

BAILE DE LOS POLLOS

The Chicken Dance

(Yucatan)

This is a dance from Yucatan, where *pollos* (chickens) form an important part of religious dance dramas. For this rhythm exercise game select a jury of four or five children. The rest of the players are rhythm dancers. They divide into two teams. Each team takes a turn at improvising the chicken dance. All the while the music plays. Some children imitate the movements of hens scratching for corn, others are hens cackling, others imitate egg laying, still others, drinking water. Some are roosters crowing or fighting or strutting proudly. While dancing, the children all chant, *"Todos somos pollos."* (We are all chickens.)

The jury, by its applause, indicates the team that has done the best improvisations and this team wins.

30

BAILE DE LOS POLLOS

Original composition by Elizabeth Colwell Nielsen

LA PUNTA Y EL TACÓN

The Tip and Heel Dance

(Cuba and Spain)

(A toe-pointing exercise for grace and rhythm)

The children form a circle and join hands. They sing the words and perform the actions in rhythm to the music. They point their toes, then balance on their heels. After one verse is sung and actions performed, they walk around in circle form as one verse of the music is played. Then they stop and sing and perform actions again.

La punta y el tacón.
Se baila con los pies.
Que a mi me lo enseño,
Mi tío Rafael.
Rafael de mi vida, y de mi corazón.
Enséñame a bailar.
La punta y el tacón.

The tip and heel
You dance with your feet,
Uncle Rafael taught me this.
Rafael, my life and heart,
Teach me to dance the
Tip and heel.

LA PUNTA Y EL TACÓN

La pun-ta y'el ta - cón. Se bai-la con los pies. Que-a mi me lo'en-se - ñó,

Mi tí - o Ra-fa - el. Ra-fa - el de mi vi - da, y de mi co - ra - zón.

En - se - ña - me'a bai - lar. La pun - ta y'el ta - cón.

Arranged by Elizabeth Colwell Nielsen

JUEGO DE LOS PAVOS

The Turkey Game

(Mexico)

A large circle is drawn on the floor or playground. Use white chalk for easy visibility or scrape the circle outline in the ground with a sharp stick.

The children are divided into two groups: *pavos* (turkeys) and *cazadores* (hunters). There should be more *pavos* than *cazadores*.

The *cazadores* and *pavos* must do a stomping step in time to music.

The *cazadores*, making the motions of strewing corn on the ground, lead the way around the circle. They must stay in time to the music.

They are followed by the children imitating *pavos*, walking or stomping in time to the music.

The *pavos* pretend to be gathering the *maíz* (corn) from the ground. They bend over as if to gobble it up.

They chant, "*Bueno, bueno, me gusta el maíz.*" (Good, good, I like the corn.)

The *cazadores* turn from time to time to try to catch the *pavos*. The *pavos* must not allow the *cazadores* to catch them. However, they must not step outside the circle to escape. Both groups keep up the stomping step to the rhythm of the music throughout the game.

If a *pavo* is caught, he retires from the game with the *cazador* who caught him.

The music continues throughout this stomping dance game until all of the children are out of the circle except one *pavo* and one *cazador*.

JUEGO DE LOS PAVOS

Play one octave lower than written throughout (both hands)

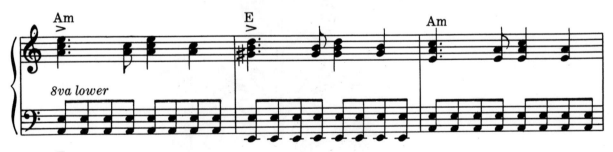

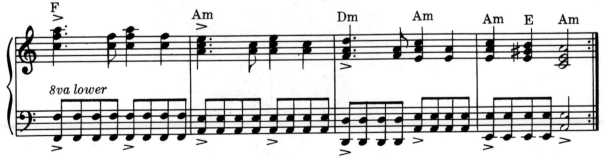

Original composition by Elizabeth Colwell Nielsen

DOS Y DOS SON CUATRO

Two and Two Are Four

(Yucatan)

A Rhythm-Clap Game

This is a counting game. The children stand in a row and clap their hands in rhythm to the music as they sing the words:

Dos y dos son cuatro,   Two and two are four,
Cuatro y dos son seis,   Four and two are six,
Seis y dos son ocho,   Six and two are eight,
Y ocho dieciseis.   And eight are sixteen.

This verse is repeated several times accompanied by the rhythmic clapping.

DOS Y DOS SON CUATRO

Lively

Dos y dos son cua - tro, Cua - tro y dos son seis,

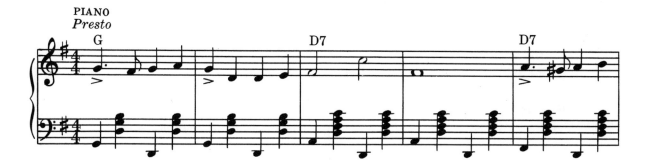

Seis y dos son o - cho, Yo - cho die - ci - seis.

PIANO
Presto

Arranged by Elizabeth Colwell Nielsen

EL MENDIGO

The Beggar

(Cuba)

This is a game that both boys and girls like. Begin by allowing the children to choose one player to be *el mendigo* (the beggar). Place the chairs in an open circle around the room. There must be a chair for every player except *el mendigo*.

El mendigo stands in the middle of the circle. He starts the game by walking over to a player and saying:

"*Dame pan y queso.*" (Give me bread and cheese.)

The player answers, "*Allá es más tieso.*" (Over there it is harder.)

As *el mendigo* goes to another player, all of the children change chairs. He attempts to get one of the chairs as the changing is taking place. If he does not get a chair on the first try, he must go to another seated player and say again, "*Dame pan y queso.*"

The child spoken to answers as before, "*Allá es más tieso.*"

Again the children change chairs. If, after a few tries, *el mendigo* does not gain a chair, he may run to the center of the circle and call, "*Todos cambian.*" (All change.)

Then all the players must change chairs while *el mendigo* watches them. This gives him a better chance to gain a chair, since he is not standing in front of or speaking to one particular child.

PRENDAS

Forfeits

(Costa Rica)

Any number of children may play this game. Each player puts a piece of his clothing or some belonging into a pile. One player is chosen to be the judge of the game and another is chosen to be the guard.

The child chosen to be the judge sits on a chair with his back to the guard so that he cannot see what the guard may be holding over his head. The player who is the guard chooses an item from the pile. The person who owns the item chosen is now called "the prisoner."

The guard holds the item over the judge's head and says, "*¿Qué tiene que hacer el prisionero para reclamarlo?*" (What must the prisoner do to redeem this?)

The judge then sentences the prisoner to do one of the following. He says:

Diga un cuento.	Tell a story.
Ladra como un perro.	Bark like a dog.
Maulla como un gato.	Meow like a cat.
Canta como un gallo.	Sing like a rooster.
Chifla como un tren.	Whistle like a train.
Brinca como un chivo.	Jump like a goat.
Vuela como un pájaro.	Fly like a bird.

The game continues until each child has had a chance to be sentenced, performed his sentence and retrieved his forfeit.

LA PIÑATA

The Piñata

(Mexico and Central America)

This game is played at birthday parties and at Christmas festivals, but is fun any time and good practice in using directional phrases.

Vaya a la izquierda.	Go to the left.
Vaya a la derecha.	Go to the right.
Más alto.	Higher.
Más bajo.	Lower.
Adelante.	Straight ahead.
Un poquito más lejos.	A little farther.
En frente de usted.	In front of you.
Detrás de usted.	Behind you.

A *piñata* is a large clay jar covered with bright-colored paper, or it is the figure of an animal made of papier-mâché. It is filled with candles and small prizes and hung from the ceiling by a cord. One child is blind-folded and tries to strike and break the *piñata* with a stick while the other children stand in a circle around him calling out directions:

"Vaya a la izquierda."	Go to the left.
"Vaya a la derecha."	Go to the right.
"Más alto."	Higher. (Etc.)

They may turn him around several times to confuse him. The blind-folded player gets three strikes. If he fails to break the *piñata*, another player gets a try. When at last one breaks it, the children all pick up the goodies and prizes that fall out.

MIENTES TÚ

You Fib

(Puerto Rico)

This is a game of progression and is useful in the study of names of fruits and vegetables.

Before beginning the game, write out, in Spanish, a list of fruits and vegetables. Elect three children to name the tricks to be done to redeem the forfeits (for example, standing on one foot while waving both arms like a bird; waving one hand while rubbing the stomach with the other; or singing a special song!). Also elect a leader to assign the name of a fruit or vegetable to each child and to collect the forfeits.

All players are seated in a group. Each player is given the name of a vegetable or fruit. One is assigned to start the game. He says, "*Anoche ví al Señor Plátano en la bodega de la esquina.*" (Last night I saw Mr. Banana in the grocery on the corner.)

Now the child whose name is Plátano says, "*Mientes tú.*" (You fib.)

"*¿Dónde estabas tú?*" (Where were you?) asks the first speaker.

"*Yo estaba en la casa de la Señora Calabaza*" (I was in the house of Mrs. Pumpkin), the child replies.

Now Señora Calabaza says to Señor Plátano, "*Mientes tú.*" (You fib.)

"*¿Dónde estabas tú?*" (Where were you?) asks Señor Plátano of Señora Calabaza.

"*Yo estaba en la casa del Señor Boniato*" (I was in the house of Mr. Sweetpotato), the child answers.

The game continues rapidly and if a player's name is mentioned and he fails to reply, then he must pay a forfeit. To pay a forfeit means that he must give on deposit something that belongs to him, such as a pencil, ring, or book. Then the game begins again.

When it is decided to end the game, each child who has paid a forfeit must perform the trick he is ordered to do to redeem his belonging.

PERRITO GOLOSO
Little Dog with a Sweet Tooth

(Cuba)

This is a game of catch. One child is chosen to be the little dog with the sweet tooth, who is called *Perrito Goloso*. This may be done by drawing slips of paper with the children's names or the game director may select a child.

The rest of the players are divided into two groups of a reasonable number, about eleven each.

The game starts by the first group asking "*¿Cuántos panes hay en el horno?*" (How many loaves of bread are in the oven?)

The second group answers, "*Veinticinco y uno quemado.*" (Twenty-five and one burned.)

"*¿Quién lo quemó?*" (Who burned it?) the first group asks.

"*El Perrito Goloso*" (The little dog with the sweet tooth), the second group replies.

"*Préndelo, préndelo*" (Catch him, catch him), all the children cry, running to catch the *perrito*.

When the *Perrito Goloso* is caught, he retires from the game and the child who caught him becomes the *perrito*. The questioning procedure is repeated.

(A *goloso* is one who likes sweets.)

JUEGO DE LA CORRIDA DE TOROS

The Bullfight Game

(Spain)

el toro	the bull
el torero	the bullfighter
la capa	the cape
los tarros (or) *cuernos*	the horns
el picador	the lancer or horseman

In every Spanish-speaking country, children play some variations of this game.

The girls are usually the spectators and cheer the principal players with calls of "hurrah" or "bravo!"

One of the boys is *el toro* and wears a pair of cardboard or wooden horns fastened to his forehead by an elastic band or string. *El torero* has a bright red piece of cloth and waves it in front of *el toro*, keeping it out of his reach.

El picador on horseback (a boy rides on a broomstick) tries to attract the attention of *el toro* away from *el torero*, who waves his red cloth close to *el toro* but has to avoid getting it caught on the horns. If *el toro* manages to butt the cloth with his horns, he wins.

ABOUT THE AUTHOR

Mariana Prieto is a resident of Florida and has lived and traveled in many Latin American countries, the West Indies, and Spain. Collecting folklore from these countries is one of her favorite hobbies. Some of the games in this book she saw played by children in the country schools of Yucatan, and others were played by her husband many years ago when he was a boy growing up in Cuba. Mrs. Prieto has taught Spanish to elementary school children; she is the author of eight previous books for children.

ABOUT THE COMPOSER-ADAPTER

Elizabeth Colwell Nielsen has long been active in the world of music. She has arranged and directed a great variety of musical programs and operettas for grades one through twelve! Mrs. Nielsen is also a resident of Florida and has taught music in the Dade County elementary, junior and senior high schools and at the University of Miami. Elizabeth Nielsen loves to write happy songs and she especially enjoyed writing and arranging the songs for the games in this book.